SCHIRMER'S LIBRARY OF MUSICAL CLASSICS

Vol. 1735

WOLFGANG AMADEUS MOZART

Original Compositions
for One Piano, Four Hands

Sonata in D, K. 381	2
Sonata in B-flat, K. 358	14
Sonata in F, K. 497	26
Sonata in C, K. 521	56
Fantasy No. 1 in F minor, K. 594	82
Fantasy No. 2 in F minor, K. 608	90
Variations in G, K. 501	100
Fugue in G minor, K. 401	108

G. SCHIRMER, Inc.

DISTRIBUTED BY

HAL•LEONARD®
CORPORATION

7777 W. BLUEMOUND RD. P.O. BOX 13819 MILWAUKEE, WI 53213

Sonata in D

W. A. Mozart, K. 381

Sonata in D

W. A. Mozart, K 381

42206 r x

Andante

Allegro molto

Allegro molto

Sonata in B♭

W. A. Mozart, K. 358

42206 r ×

Sonata in B♭

Allegro

W. A. Mozart, K. 358

PRIMO

Adagio

Sonata in F

W. A. Mozart, K. 497

42206 r x

Composed in 1786.

Sonata in F

W. A. Mozart, K. 497

Allegro

Sonata in C

W. A. Mozart, K. 521

Sonata in C

W. A. Mozart, K. 521

Andante

42206

Allegretto

73

42206

Fantasy No.1 in F minor

W. A. Mozart, K. 594

Adagio

42206 r x   Composed in 1790

Fantasy No.1 in F minor

W. A. Mozart, K. 594

Allegro

Fantasy No. 2 in F minor

W. A. Mozart, K. 608

Composed in 1791

Fantasy No. 2 in F minor

W. A. Mozart, K. 608

Allegro

42206 r x

Theme and Variations in G

42206 r x   Composed in 1786

Theme and Variations in G

W. A. Mozart, K. 501

Var. III

Var. III

106

42206

Fugue in G minor

W. A. Mozart, K. 401

Fugue in G minor

W. A. Mozart, K. 401

42206 г x